HALO OF MORNING

Halo of Morning

poems by Glen Sorestad

Leaf Press
Lantzville, Canada
2006

Library and Archives Canada Cataloguing in Publication

Sorestad, Glen A., 1937-
    Halo of morning / Glen Sorestad.

Poems.
ISBN 0-9780536-5-6

    I. Title.
PS8587.O746H34 2006   C811'.54   C2006-905815-6

We are grateful for permission to use the cover photograph by Greg Pond, whose work is shown at www.flickr.com/photos/greg7.

"Morning Declaration" appeared in *Fieldstone* (an online literary journal), and both "Crisp October Morning" and "Grebe Dance" appeared on the Leaf Press Monday's Poem web page (the latter with a different title).

The text of this chapbook is printed on paper made of 100% post-consumer waste and produced by wind power.

Leaf Press
P.O. Box 416
Lantzville, B.C., Canada V0R 2H0
www.leafpress.ca

The problem is how to look intelligent
with our mouths agape ...

Stephen Dunn

Contents

The First Robin

is perched atop the roof peak,
gaudy orange breast
spinning a small sun at us
as it trills its thrushy tune
with apt exuberance,
declaiming its territory
for all to hear,
its operatic presence
on this April day
like a welcome banner
slung before our eyes.

After Five Days of North Wind

the Red-winged Blackbird
emerges sun-dazed
from deep in tall reeds
where it has alternated
shivering and calling out
a wind-weakened spring trill,
albeit without its usual gusto.

Today it perches atop
the pale green glimmer
of new-leafed aspen beneath
an endless azure dazzle,
and greets us with a burst
of exuberant territorial song,
as happy to be freed from
the frigid winds as we.

Grebe Dance

The first pair of Red-necked Grebes
I've seen this year are on the pond
as I step along the gravel path,
the park walk my morning ritual.
It is spring, the sun is warm.

I cross the small causeway
that divides the pond and see
them swim towards each other,
then rise up from the water,
breast to breast, beak to beak,
their feet furious paddles
propelling them upright
in this showy water ballet.

I am of no consequence here.
It is spring, the sun is warm,
and Nature, everywhere, urges
these annual rites, dances
that sing the mystery of life,
the promise of the season.

Halo of Morning

The awakening sky
is a splendid halo
we wear as we walk.

Dew-fresh air parts,
allowing us to bear
the pale light

of morn like Magi
come from the east,
this sky our gift.

Morning Declaration

This morning the northwest wind blusters
a declarative sentence replete with clausal
gusts punctuated with rainy exclamations.

The golf course is a silent thought;
even omnipresent Canada Geese have
opted not to declare their plaintive intents,

gone to seek shelter somewhere beyond
utterance. Trees shake their leaves
like pompom quotation marks.

Those in subordinate servitude to dogs
have been taken out, thoroughly roused
and returned safe to their warm homes.

My partner and I, who persist in a fitness
imperative, lean, two slashes into the rain
and follow our syntactical route home.

Heat

It is six a.m. and already the sun
begins to blow-torch the earth.
The white-tailed jack rabbit,
too languid to leap in alarm,
hunkers low in the grass
and tries its best to disappear.

A lone white vapour trail
mars a doldrum azure sea,
a brilliance that calls out the shades.
I feel sweat start its slow trickle
down my forehead, my neck
and we are only halfway home.

Two men in T-shirts and shorts
jog towards us, faces streaming.
By the time we reach our door
we'll be as shiny as they are now.
Turn on the air-conditioning
and draw the drapes—
summer is here this morning.

The First Yellow Leaf

I was not ready for it. Before me the elm leaf,
unwanted harbinger, lay on the cement walk.

I glared up as if to chastise the offending tree
and that's when I noticed there were more,

many more, an abundant gilding of what was
so lately green. Precursor, this lone leaf,

as much as I am unprepared; as much as I
may huff and get my back up against the fact;

as much as I may decry the sudden way I was
blind-sided, oblivious to the obvious; without

my recognition and as surely whether I
appeal or not, the seasons fly, the seasons fly.

What the Geese Say

September morning, bright sky.
I hear them in the distance,
drawing closer—Canada Geese.
A raucous flock, perhaps
two dozen, a raggedy-ass formation
of new recruits passes overhead,
an insult to all those
smartly turned-out orderly vees.
And I think this disorderly
flying mob consists mainly of juveniles
with parents doing their best to urge order
from this flapping chaos. They pass above
in louder-than-usual dissonance
that sounds very much to my ear
like the goose-equivalents of:
  Are we there yet?
  When do we get to eat?
  How much further?
  Mom, Janey's giving me that look!

And somehow it all seems
so familiar and I remember
threatening to stop the car,
to let the combatants out
to walk for a while. Or driving
once all the way from Vancouver
to Calgary because the kids wouldn't shut up.

The geese veer unexpectedly off
their flight path, swing a large arc
and then wing back over us again
on their previous bearing. I have
the distinct sense that this time
there is decidedly less goose-whining,
and the formation much tauter—
what might almost be recognizable
as a goose-norm. As they disappear
I have this feeling Canada Geese
will still be flying when the Earth's
last human is returned to dust.

Woman with Two Dogs

We always offer "Good Morning"
to the woman leashed to two dogs
as we meet her somewhere along
the park path. She always answers,

but her face can never mask her
displeasure at being the one who
must rise to take the small beasts
for their early morning rite.

It is clear she did not choose
her companions: her partner, perhaps
the children were responsible
and now it seems she has earned

through some elimination dance
the dubious pleasure the others have
forgone for whatever reasons.
This is not the way her day would

start were she the one to choose.
But she does what she must, takes
the wagging twosome for ablutions,
though mustering a smile is hard.

Crisp October Morning

I step out into a world of frost—
not a thin hint, but layered
as a long-neglected freezer,
exaggerating each grass blade.

A delicious shiver of sky,
raucous clamour of Snow Geese
writing their delicate poem,
wavering white lines on blue.

My breath jets words I
can not call back, or even
recognize, as I butt my way
against the morning cold.

Mallards in the park have
paddled the sub-zero night
and kept open a patch of pond,
the rest skinned with ice.

Late Heron

It is November and large white flakes
fall soft as breath as we tread the path
between the park's two ponds. Motionless

beside the only open water stands
a Great Blue Heron, forlorn in the float
of wet flakes. Does the bird know

it is an anachronism of the month,
obtrusive against a wintry backdrop?
Perhaps the bird is wounded; or old and weak

it sees its fate reflected in the still water
and simply waits out its remaining time—
falling prey to sharp teeth or winter cold.

Its kin, long flown to warmer pools,
are receding memories. Silent snow
falls on the heron, falls on us.

Old Man & Dog

In awakening sub-zero light November
is flaking the air with snow.
Tendril wisps undulate across the path
when I spot the slow pair
we often greet in the park.

Today the old man is garbed
in heavy winter coat, wool scarf
and furry hat; the small white pooch
nattily attired in green & white
plaid jacket, jaunty collar turned up,
as if off to a sporting event.

It is winter now, much as
we'd like to deny it, and it
would be much more comfortable
to have stayed inside.
But the two old timers
brunt winter's worst together
and this thought warms me,
long after I have passed.

November Is

an old lamp that needs
a new bulb; a favourite jacket
that needs a fleece lining;
that storm door you meant
to buy last summer on sale;
a pile of unraked leaves
slumped in a winter wait;
the snow tires you forgot
to buy and need today;
a solitary watering can
on an apartment balcony.

November is an endless stream
of headlight beams at eight a.m.;
the clatter-dance of aspens
in a northwest wind-lament;
a magical meringue of frost,
trees hoary spectres;
an ice-cloud that sleeps
in the city overnight;
the black and white silence
of magpie against frozen sky.

Late November

First light muscles its way
between the condos of Highland Place.
I stride down Heritage Crescent,
shake the cold hand of the half-dark.
Icy breath of dawn wind lurks
at my back, but when I arc my way
past the ponds and turn homewards
in twenty minutes, the wind will
crack its knuckles, clutch for any
exposed skin; its frigid fingers will
slap my cheeks ruddy, sneak under
my glasses, turn on the nasal faucet.

Of course, I could walk indoors
round and round the mall's perimeter
like all the other mall amblers
(like a wolf in a glassed-in pen)
where I need no mitts, no toque,
no fleece or down-filled coat,
where no snow or ice will
trick my step and catapult me
into a cartoon character.

But I much prefer the crick
and crunch of my shoes
on a snowy gravel path,
a live uncommercial landscape
with air that moves, that fills
the lungs with a stirring smell
of time past and the heady
scent of time to come.

Towards the Long Night

It seems but a short time ago that we
walked at six a.m. and already the sun
was high in the sky, the day warmed.

Now in late November we wait later
each morning for light, the tardy sun
dragging its school-bound feet.

It is after eight and Old Sol has
still not tossed back all the blankets
from his eastern bed, though worldly shapes

emerge from the dark like dreams.
The sharp sting of wind in our faces,
we drag slow light through the park.

December Sun

Each morning the sun
rises further south,
skates a smaller portion
of the great blue rink.
It is after nine
and we have walked
over half our route
in toothy sub-zero frost
to this corner where
we turn east, turn our faces
to the just-waking sun,
its puny rays that can
no longer melt snow.

We step into the spreading
glow, weak as it is,
that bathes the horizon
in pinks and mauves,
and makes of the east
a painter's sky we'd love
to hang on one of our walls.